# The Girls' Handbook of Spells

✴

# The Girls' Handbook of Spells

Charm your way to
popularity and power!

ANTONIA BEATTIE

**REWARD BOOKS**

# Contents

# Introduction ~ Good and Bad Spells

Spells have been a part of life since the earliest days of human existence. There are countless spells, both recorded on paper and passed down by word of mouth, that have been designed to help the spell caster attract love, luck and popularity. There have also been spells that have helped shield the spell caster and their loved ones from disaster and failure.

There are good spells and bad spells. This book is concerned with good spells — those spells that can be safely performed for your benefit or that of your family and friends. Bad spells, that is, those that try to harm or to make a person do things against their will, are particularly dangerous and are ones to steer well clear of. Apart from reasons of decency, bad spells attract three times the amount of negative energy that is being sent out.

Spells are merely a way of collecting, raising and directing energy. There is a belief that there is a great amount of psychic energy circulating in our bodies. This energy can link into the psychic energy of the Earth. Spellcraft is essentially Earth magic. Spells help you tap into the psychic energy within you and the Earth so that you can harness it to create a new reality where your wish will become real.

By sending out energy to attract happiness, popularity or some other positive outcome, you are sending out a flare that will attract more of that particular type of positive energy to you. Spells give an extra push to make things happen in your favor, and help rearrange the type of energy that is flowing to you.

If what you want feels beyond your reach, spells can help attract to you the opportunities you can follow to reach your desired goal. They can also help to give you the ability to recognize these opportunities, and are an excellent way of strengthening your intuition.

However, spellcraft should not be used as a substitute for doing all you can physically and mentally to make things happen in your life. Working at getting what you want is also part of your own personal magic and can actually be very helpful in gathering in the information that will make your spell casting even more powerful and successful.

Spells are built largely around herbs, candles and perfumes. Traditionally, none of the tools used were ever expensive or difficult to obtain. The spells and charms in this book use readily available ingredients and tools found at home — herbs, candles, needles, thread, crystal and other things you probably have already. A lot of space, time and money are unnecessary for creating some very powerful spells. But you must have faith in yourself, and a deep inner belief that you can attain your desired end.

Enjoy being creative with your spell casting. Experiment with the different spells in this handbook and discover which ones work best for you. Spell casting can be used as your own way of learning how to work with other people and the Earth on a deeply spiritual level. As you develop your intuition, you will find you are automatically using certain types of herbs and oils in your own tailor made spells. It is then that you will weave the most potent magic of all.

# Spellcraft ~ Getting Your Head Together

## What are spells?

A spell is a way of focusing your mind to get what you want. By concentrating all your energy on what you want to have or to make happen, you can bring about changes to your life. Spellcraft is a way of making the changes happen on a psychic level. Once the change is made on this level, you will find it easier to achieve changes at the level of reality. Why?

There are many aspects of life that cannot be controlled, and spells are often useful when you are faced with a situation in which you don't quite know what to do. Spells help you tap into a greater force than yourself. This force is known as Earth energy — the largest source of psychic energy we know.

Once the psychic change is achieved by doing a spell, you will find strange coincidences happen that help your wish to become reality. Coincidences are often an indication that magic is happening around you. Doing a spell is like setting up a beacon in the cosmos to attract help or a particular form of energy to you.

There are many different types of spells. Some use traditional words or phrases that have evolved over time. Other spells use traditional tools, such as different colored candles. Linking into these traditions often helps the spell to work, because words or actions repeated again and again seem to build up their own energy over time. However, just as often the best spells are the ones you create for yourself.

# How do spells work?

Spells work best when performed after you have:
  * worked out exactly what you want to do;
  * imagined in great detail how things will change;
  * allowed yourself to be guided by your intuition and personal knowledge;
  * convinced yourself that you can make a difference.

Spells don't work when you have a deep seated feeling that you don't deserve the things you want. For longer lasting results, work out how to get rid of any such self-defeating feelings, and discover your own individual path to happiness. For quicker results, consider working with a group of friends, and cast spells for each other.

Nor do spells work fully if you are not tapped into the psychic energy of the Earth. To be grounded and centered is the best way of ensuring that your spell will work. Follow the exercise on pages 28–29.

Spells are often a mixture of words, objects and actions that are chosen so that their vibrations tune into your purpose. For example, if you want to find a new love, you would traditionally use ingredients such as red candle, patchouli oil, rose quartz and the petals of a red rose. By focusing on preparing the spell and by saying a series of words over and over again, you are creating a powerful spell to find a new love.

Over time, various stones, animals, birds, trees, plants and colors have been given certain magical meanings. These are sometimes called associations or correspondences, and this book will give you some of the most common correspondences for various spells.

Spellcraft ~ Getting Your Head Together

11

# What do you want to do?

One of the most important elements of spellcraft is to know what you want. Be careful what you ask for. Do not be tempted to tamper with another person's free will as this is getting close to black magic.

Many traditional spells were aimed at making another person fall in love with the magician or witch, irrespective of the intended lover's will, or of conjuring spirits to entice the girl/boy to come to the magician or witch. Many magicians and witches paid a heavy price for such coercive behavior, including death (see pages 16–17). The best love or friendship spells are those that do not name a person, but allow the cosmos to choose the best friend or love for you (see "Finding new friends" on pages 42–43 and "Falling in and out of love" on pages 52–59).

One of the most important aspects of spellcraft is its emphasis on the need to follow your true will. In many magical traditions, a person's true will is always attuned to their greater good, and not just to doing whatever they feel like. Your true will is always what feels "right" to you. If you get an uneasy feeling about any spell, this is a clear sign that you must not do it. It is important that you follow your true feelings rather than mere whims.

To get a positive result with your spellcraft you need to focus clearly on the outcome you want. But you must also give yourself time to think through the result of the spell (see "Helping friends in need" on pages 44–45).

Some traditional spells come from books, while others are handed down through folklore. Use the spells in this Handbook as examples of the types of spells you can weave for yourself. It is often best to tailor your spells to your individual circumstances, using various "tools" that can be found in nature or made from natural substances, such as beeswax or 100 per cent palm oil (see "Candles" on pages 18–19), semiprecious stones (see "Stones of power" on pages 20–21), cotton or silk threads (see "Fabric and thread" on page 22), and trees and leaves (see pages 24–25).

Much of Western magic is based on the belief that there are four basic elements, such as earth, air, fire and water. Many ancient civilizations believed that the world was made up of a combination of elements and that these elements create magic when combined correctly.

| Element | Tools symbolizing the element in spellcraft | Aspects of life symbolizing the element |
|---------|---------------------------------------------|------------------------------------------|
| Earth | Stones | Your body and the material things around you, like money and home |
| Air | Burning incense sticks | Your ability to think |
| Fire | Candles | Your will, passion and creativity |
| Water | Bowls of water | Your emotions |

Spellcraft ~ Getting Your Head Together

# Making spells happen

To empower a spell, you need to learn the art of concentration. You need to visualize your spell's success. If you cast a spell for attracting a new friend, for instance, you could visualize yourself sitting with your new friend and imagine feeling happy and content with your new friendship. If you are looking for a job, imagine an envelope with a nice healthy pay check inside.

If you notice that your mind starts to wander when you are trying to visualize the successful outcome of your spell, it might be worthwhile to do a few visualization exercises. These exercises are simple, but they do take a great deal of concentration. However, the effort quickly pays off (see pages 30–31).

To cast a spell successfully, you must believe not only that the spell can work, but also that you personally can make the change happen. Feeling empowered to make changes is one of the most important keys to successful spellcraft.

One way to feel a sense of your power and your ability to make a difference is to tap into the psychic energy of the Earth. The following exercise will help you to feel the Earth's power.

Sit comfortably on the floor or ground, close your eyes and imagine yourself as a tree. The first step is to concentrate on your spine as you are sitting, starting from the base and working, bit by bit, up to the base of your skull, feeling the flow of energy through your body. Imagine that your spine is illuminated in a golden light. Then turn that golden light into a golden trunk of a tree.

Visualize the base of your golden trunk extending downward into the earth. Let your mind drift free as you watch the roots grow and spread, anchoring your body into the earth. Imagine your branches rising up and flowing gracefully down, to touch the ground like those of a willow tree.

Feel the throb of the energy pulsing through you. Feel yourself capable of doing anything you want. When you're ready, shut down the color and focus on your breathing. After a while the image will fade but you should allow the feeling of being connected to remain. By being connected to the earth, you are in a better position to fulfill your potential.

Spellcraft ~ Getting Your Head Together

# Some important magical rules

The spells included in this Handbook are all beneficial in nature. It is important to remember the traditional law of Magic: "If it harm none, do what you will". You must be very careful, when deciding what spell to cast, that you do not act selfishly or try to hurt anyone.

If you do hurt someone with your spell, even without meaning to, you will have to deal with a kind of karma. Karma is an Eastern concept of paying for the wrong you do to others. The same thing happens in Western Magic: here the belief is that whatever is sent out returns in time upon the sender. In Western magic, the formula is said to be "that which is sent out returns threefold".

Sometimes it is legitimate that a spell is worked to bind someone from doing harm to others. White witches have been known to work such magic when it is thought to be for the greater good. However, there is always a price to be paid. During the Second World War, a group of witches cast spells to prevent Hitler from invading England. A worthy purpose, but some of the witches who were involved in the spells died soon after the ritual. They were quite elderly, and some people feel that they were willingly making the ultimate sacrifice for their country.

It is also important not to force anyone to do your bidding. You are wasting a lot of energy if the person is not interested. It needs a lot of energy to actually pull off such a spell, and this is possibly one reason past magicians needed to call up certain spirits to coerce a person into doing something they do not wish to do. However, the magician usually had to pay a heavy price — these spirits tended to charge quite heavily for their services.

Although there is really no set path for casting spells, consider incorporating the basics of good magical practices, in the following order:

* find or make the right tools for your spellcraft (see pages 18–25);
* learn how to feel your own natural power (see pages 28–29);
* find or create a special place where you can feel comfortable and safe (see pages 34–35);
* learn how to time your spells (see pages 38–39);
* use the spells in this Handbook with goodwill and good intention.

# Spellcraft Tools

## Candles

andles are often very important in spells. Wax was considered an essential tool for witches, who used it to mold symbols of their wishes and curses. Today it is believed that wax candles can hold any magical intention, and spells are an example. Some spells require that you choose a particular color for your candle or advise rubbing oil over the candle or carving a short version of your wish on the candle itself. The color, oil and carvings will enhance your magical wish. Once the candle is burnt, your magical wish is released into the cosmos. Candles are also useful for helping you focus on your magical intention. They are now commercially available in many colors, shapes and sizes.

Choose a colored candle that will help you focus on what you wish to happen. Choose the color of your candle according to your intuition or by selecting one that vibrates with your purpose.

| Color of candle | Corresponding meaning | Corresponding oil |
|-----------------|----------------------|-------------------|
| Red | Love | Patchouli |
| Pink | Friendship | Mugwort |
| Orange | Courage | Endive |
| Green | Money | Cinnamon |
| Yellow/gold | Confidence | Basil |
| Blue | Calm | Chamomile |
| Purple | Power | Frankincense |

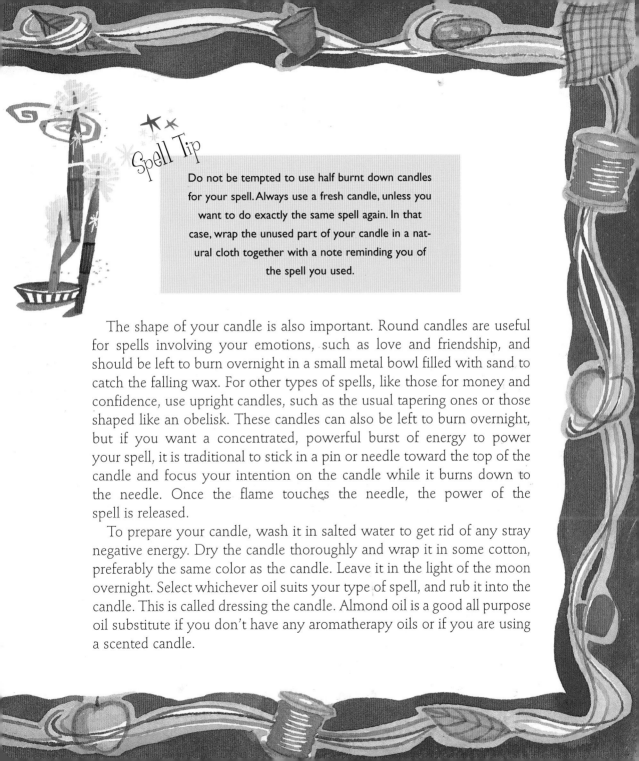

Do not be tempted to use half burnt down candles for your spell. Always use a fresh candle, unless you want to do exactly the same spell again. In that case, wrap the unused part of your candle in a natural cloth together with a note reminding you of the spell you used.

The shape of your candle is also important. Round candles are useful for spells involving your emotions, such as love and friendship, and should be left to burn overnight in a small metal bowl filled with sand to catch the falling wax. For other types of spells, like those for money and confidence, use upright candles, such as the usual tapering ones or those shaped like an obelisk. These candles can also be left to burn overnight, but if you want a concentrated, powerful burst of energy to power your spell, it is traditional to stick in a pin or needle toward the top of the candle and focus your intention on the candle while it burns down to the needle. Once the flame touches the needle, the power of the spell is released.

To prepare your candle, wash it in salted water to get rid of any stray negative energy. Dry the candle thoroughly and wrap it in some cotton, preferably the same color as the candle. Leave it in the light of the moon overnight. Select whichever oil suits your type of spell, and rub it into the candle. This is called dressing the candle. Almond oil is a good all purpose oil substitute if you don't have any aromatherapy oils or if you are using a scented candle.

# Stones of power

Like candles, precious and semiprecious stones hold magical vibrations that correspond with our emotions and desires. Precious stones include diamonds, rubies and sapphires. Semiprecious stones include moonstones and amethysts; there are many semiprecious stones that are effective for money, love and other types of spells.

If you are looking for a stone to help power a spell, a great way of finding the right stone for your purpose is to visit your favorite stone shop or park and pick up the first rock you see while thinking about your spell. Your intuition will often help you find the right stone. If no stone makes its presence felt, then don't use a stone for your spell.

As you collect your stones, cleanse them with salt water or in a natural stream to remove any negative vibrations. If you enjoy using stones and seem to have a few of them about, store them in a special box or basket, preferably lined with natural material such as cotton, silk, flax or hemp, to keep them safe. Include in your box a list of your stones and any useful information about them.

Stones are often useful in protection spells or charm bags, where you can carry the stone with you, letting it attract your wish to you constantly. Charm bags can contain a special word, image, herb and stone. If you were making a charm bag for a friendship spell, it might contain a heart-shaped piece of rose quartz, whereas a charm bag for a money spell, might contain a green-colored stone, such as a piece of jade.

Spellcraft Tools

The table below will help you to choose a stone. However, if you are still in doubt as to what stone to use, settle for a piece of clear quartz crystal. This stone is very useful in all types of spells and other magical practices.

| Stone | Magical properties |
| --- | --- |
| Agate | improves energy |
| Amber | encourages good fortune |
| Amethyst | improves a sense of your true beauty |
| Aquamarine | strengthens inspiration |
| Bloodstone | relieves depression |
| Garnet | encourages friendships |
| Jade | attracts wealth |
| Jasper | protects against nightmares |
| Lapis lazuli | relieves trauma |
| Malachite | increases a sense of health |
| Moonstone | attracts friendships and emotional strength |
| Obsidian (black) | releases old negative feelings |
| Obsidian (green) | protects from difficult people |
| Pearl | releases anger |
| Tourmaline | wins friends |
| Turquoise | protects against negative actions |

Spellcraft Tools

# Fabric and thread

In any spell, it is important to use only natural objects, because they hold magical power much more easily than artificially made objects such as nylon and plastic. Fabric often features in the making of charm bags or the storing of your magical tools. Try to use only cotton, silk, flax, hemp and other natural fabrics. The same holds true for threads — use only wool, cotton or silk threads.

Some of the most effective spells use cord magic. For this type of magic, all you need is a length of rope or cord into which you can knot your magical intention.

## Traditional Spell

Take a cord long enough to be knotted nine times (for example, 27 inches (69 cm), depending on the thickness of your cord) and say the following words and make the knots in the following pattern, while concentrating on the success of your spell:

*By knot of one, the spell's begun.*

*By knot of two, it comes true.*

*By knot of three, so mote it be.*

*By knot of four, power I store.*

*By knot of five, the spell is alive.*

*By knot of six, the spell is fixed.*

*By knot of seven, events I'll leaven.*

*By knot of eight, it will be Fate.*

*By knot of nine, what is done is mine.*

# Trees and leaves

Branches, bark and leaves of trees can be very useful for a number of different types of spells. For advanced magic, wands that help focus psychic energy can be made from powerful types of wood. Traditionally, ash is the best wood for a magic wand. However, in simpler types of spells, a piece of wood can be included in a charm bag or simply carried in your pocket or wallet to attract a certain form of energy.

| Type of wood | Magical use |
| --- | --- |
| Almond | attracts a loyal love |
| Ash | protects from negative energies |
| Birch | heightens psychic energy |
| Cedar | attracts money |
| Dogwood | protects secrets |
| Elm | aids communication |
| Holly | improves friendships |
| Mistletoe | protects against negative energy |
| Oak | attracts good luck |
| Rowan | attracts creativity |
| Willow | aids all forms of healing |

The leaves of some of these trees can also be used in your spells. For example, the leaf of an ash tree placed somewhere safe on your bicycle or in your car can protect you from accidents. Use a leaf of the dogwood in your diary to keep it safe from prying eyes.

When you are finding pieces of wood for your spells, it is best if your wood has already separated from the tree; for example a branch may have been blown off a tree by high winds or broken by a lightning strike.

Spellcraft Tools

# Traditional Spell

Do not break branches, bark or leaves off a tree. If you do, you will find that your spell will not be very effective.

Small blocks or strips of wood that you can get from a hardware store, like pine or balsa, can also be used for spells. Pine can be used for healing spells. For example, you can write on a thin sliver of pine board the name of the person to whom you wish to send healing energies. You may wish to draw happy images around the person's name or a runic symbol such as a ( ᛈ ), symbolizing comfort and pleasure. Balsa is useful for sending all sorts of psychic energy, so you can use this wood in protection charms.

## Spellcraft Tools

# Feeling Powerful

## Preparing yourself for spellcraft

To do any spell successfully, the first step is to clear everyday things from your thoughts.

Having a bath or shower before you do any spells is a very effective way of clearing away all the troubles of the day prior to doing some magical work.

If you are having a shower, stand directly under the shower head and imagine your body being encased by the water, which is removing all the troubles or unhappiness or even just the thoughts of the day. At this

point, do not even think about your spell. All you need to do is clear your mind and get a sense of stillness. Watch the water swirling down the drain together with your everyday thoughts.

If you are having a bath, you could do a cleansing visualization with a lighted candle while lying in the tub. Place a beeswax candle or tea light where it can be seen safely and easily from the bathtub. Also place a large glass of cool water where you can easily reach it from the tub.

| Aromatherapy oil | Qualities |
| --- | --- |
| Cedarwood | stabilizes emotions |
| Geranium | cleanses emotions |
| Lavender | attracts calmness |
| Lovage | attracts love |
| Marjoram | relieves grief |
| Peppermint | overcomes shock |
| Sandalwood | stimulates confidence |
| Vervain/Verbena | attracts lover |
| Ylang ylang | relieves depression |

As you soak in the water (to which you have added some sea salt and perhaps a drop or two of an essential oil — see the table above), take the time to feel the effects on your senses. Check the taste in your mouth, taking a sip of water if you feel a little thirsty. Notice the scent of the oils you have chosen, create little waves in your tub with your hands and listen to the motion of the water, experiencing the way the hot and cold water of your bath are mingling and caressing your skin. Allow your eyes to stare momentarily at the lighted candle. Close your eyes and imagine the candle flame in the middle of your forehead, your "third eye". Hold the image for as long as possible and then relax with your eyes closed. Imagine any stray thoughts floating away from your head in a bubble.

When you are ready, get out of the bath or the shower and dry yourself with a fresh towel. Let the water out and watch all your worries and everyday thoughts go down the drain with it.

# Mirror magic ~ helping you ground and center yourself

Mirror magic is a great way of helping boost your self-confidence and self-esteem and is easy to carry out. All you need is a full length mirror.

After your bath or shower, stand in front of the mirror with your feet together. Feel your shoulder blades drop and allow your shoulders to straighten and your chest to rise, freeing any constriction on your diaphragm. Check particularly how your back feels. If your lower back feels stressed while you are standing, tilt your pelvis forward by bending your knees slightly.

Look at yourself in the mirror. Try to gain some distance from any negative judgments about yourself by imagining a line of energy running through the middle of your body. Visualize that line of energy going down your legs, past your feet and into the ground under the floorboards. Then imagine another line of energy coming up from the earth into your body. As you breathe in, see the energy coming up from the earth through your body looping above your head and, as you breathe out, see the energy go back down into the ground, where it loops somewhere below your feet to come back through your body (see the picture on page 15). Concentrate on your breathing. Keep visualizing this energy moving

Feeling Powerful

through and around you and that the lines of energy are getting stronger and thicker until they are like cords. This is called grounding.

Use the mirror to help you straighten your body along this central line of energy. Without moving any limbs, imagine all the muscles in your body moving toward this center, balancing your body. Attempt to feel the muscles in the front of your legs pushing back against those in the back of your legs and then try from the sides pushing inward. Imagine this feeling traveling up the trunk of your body into your mind. Focus your mind on the glowing lines of energy that are feeding your body and mind with new energy with every breath you take while taking away old energy with every breath you exhale. This is an excellent exercise to do both before and after you have cast your spell.

Spell Tip

When we feel ugly, stupid or socially undesirable, this most often means that our energy is disconnected from the earth. If you feel like this, try to do this exercise, even if you are not planning to do any spells. It is important to stay connected with the earth to help get rid of feelings of depression and unhappiness.

# Learning to focus

Visualizing something that isn't there is sometimes not an easy thing to do. Playing with your imagination requires concentration and time. Some people can visualize easily, but most need to practice.

Try focusing on a photograph of something you can stand staring at for a while, like a poster. Notice all the details, such as the shape of things in the background. Once you feel confident that you know the picture well, tear the photograph in half. Put one half on the table in front of you and try to visualize the other half.

As an advanced exercise, imagine your favorite food and use all your senses — see it, touch it, smell it, eat it, and hear the crunch or squish as you bite into it.

Visualization is an important part of spell casting. Gathering the ingredients you need for your spell, putting them together in the right proportions and muttering the rights words are important elements in setting up your spell. With visualization, you will be able to power your spell more forcefully.

When you are making all your preparations for your spell, no matter whether you are only going to the store to buy a stone to carry in your pocket for good luck or protection, you should enhance the spell with a visualization. For example, to empower your purchase of the right stone for protection, visualize the stone's ability to protect you. Do this by imagining someone coming up to you wanting to do you harm, but not being able to see you any more.

If you notice that your mind starts to wander when you are trying to visualize the success of your spell, it might be worthwhile to do a bit more visualization practice. Also, if the spell is for yourself, you might be subconsciously sabotaging your spell by feeling in some way unworthy of success. Take time to understand any negative thoughts you may have about the success you seek. If you are not 100 per cent behind your spell, it will not work.

Continue to work on understanding why you don't want your spell to work. At the same time, consider asking someone you trust to do the spell for you (see pages 44–45). Sometimes, once the spell has been cast, you may get some further inspiration on how to rid yourself of your negative feelings, and this may clear the way for you to do the spell next time.

Feeling Powerful

# Making a spell box for yourself

Spell boxes can be used for any type of special spell. They can be put together as presents for your friends or as protection for your home. By making a spell box for yourself, you are creating a strong image of who you are. Knowing who you really are is very powerful magic and is an excellent protection against people who are very critical toward you or unappreciative of you. Your own spell box will allow you to focus your imagination on what you are and what you want to be. It is your magical identity kit.

You will first need a box, preferably made from metal, wood or paper. It should be about 6 inches (15 cm) wide, between 4 inches (10 cm) and 6 inches deep and up to 6 inches tall. The lid of the box can be hinged or loose. Decorate your box with your favorite paper, colors and images. You can paint your box, glue pebbles or stones on it, line fabric inside it and use raffia or a cord with a tassel to bind it so that no one looks into it.

Once your box is ready and you are pleased with the way it looks, add the following ingredients:

* a small snipping of your hair;
* a symbol of an eye with the pupil the same color as your eyes;
* some actual nail clippings (if you like wearing a particular color of nail polish, cut out the shape of your nails from a piece of balsa wood and paint it white, and then layer it with your favorite nail enamel);
* your favorite perfumes or aromatherapy oils (sprinkled on some natural fabric);
* your favorite types of stone;
* an example of your favorite things to do (a piece of your embroidery, a string from your guitar, or a drill bit);
* a picture of your favorite, or favorite types of, food; and
* a note, on some parchment like paper, about when you like to eat, for how long you like to sleep, what part of your body feels strong and what type of thinking you like doing (for example, whether you like making up rhymes, whether you are able to do mental arithmetic in your head fairly easily).

Include all these things in your box, as well as anything else you feel will identify who you truly are. As you gather your ingredients, keep thinking of yourself as a strong, balanced person who can create whatever you truly need in your life. Keep this box somewhere safe. It is not to be shown to anyone; make it purely for yourself. Some things won't stay the same, so feel free to change some of the objects in your spell box as you change.

Feeling Powerful

# Where and When

## Preparing your space for spellcraft

The best place to do your spell casting is within a space or Circle that is quiet and protected from interruptions, and creates a distance from the worries of the real world, linking you with another world where you can tap into a deeper source of energy. To do the best spells you need to work between the worlds.

To set up your space for spellcraft, take a private area in your home, whether it is your bedroom, study, workshop or garden, and set up a little table. Upon it, you can place some flowers, candles, incense and a bowl half full of sand. Ensure that the table is big enough for you to work on your spells and write them up in a journal.

Keep this area aside for spell casting and make sure that no clutter starts to build up. If clutter does become a problem, hang or place a clear quartz crystal where the clutter is worst, and let the stone clear the energy in the area and remind you to keep it tidy.

Imagine as wide a Circle as your area allows you. Put a compass in the middle of your Circle and check out where north is (if you are

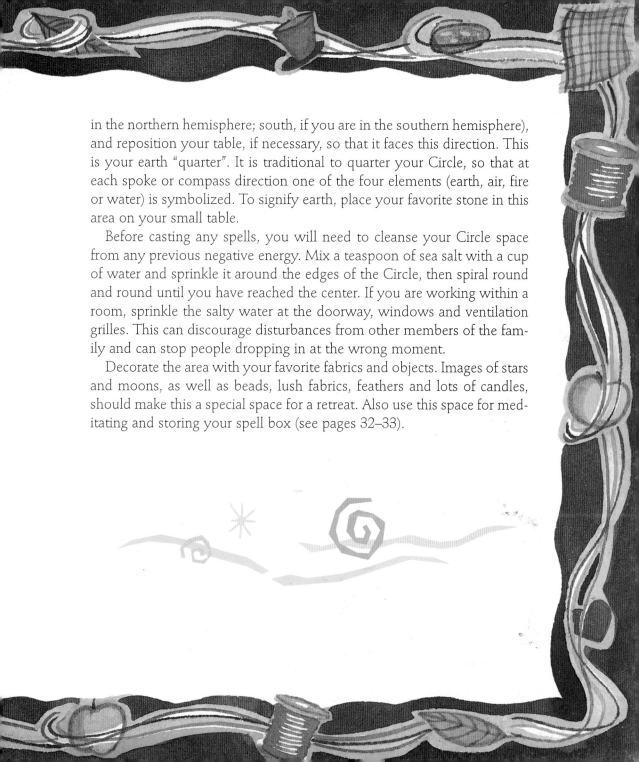

in the northern hemisphere; south, if you are in the southern hemisphere), and reposition your table, if necessary, so that it faces this direction. This is your earth "quarter". It is traditional to quarter your Circle, so that at each spoke or compass direction one of the four elements (earth, air, fire or water) is symbolized. To signify earth, place your favorite stone in this area on your small table.

Before casting any spells, you will need to cleanse your Circle space from any previous negative energy. Mix a teaspoon of sea salt with a cup of water and sprinkle it around the edges of the Circle, then spiral round and round until you have reached the center. If you are working within a room, sprinkle the salty water at the doorway, windows and ventilation grilles. This can discourage disturbances from other members of the family and can stop people dropping in at the wrong moment.

Decorate the area with your favorite fabrics and objects. Images of stars and moons, as well as beads, lush fabrics, feathers and lots of candles, should make this a special space for a retreat. Also use this space for meditating and storing your spell box (see pages 32–33).

# Working between the worlds

The Circle is a very powerful symbol of infinity, unity and the cycle of the Seasons. Spells should ideally be cast within a Circle. By creating a Circle, you will be able to protect yourself from any harmful presences and concentrate the power that you are raising for your spell.

Collect all your ingredients for your spell and place them in your special space. Get absolutely everything you need. Once you have cast your Circle, you must not break it until you have finished your spell. If you are desperate to go to the bathroom, you may cut a doorway in the Circle by making a swift, cutting motion with your hand from above your head toward (and touching) the floor at the edge of your Circle.

Where and When

Never cross the boundaries of your Circle once it has been
cast unless you cut a doorway in the Circle. Remember
always to close the doorway behind you.
To open your Circle at the end of the spell casting, imagine that
you are reeling in a blue cord. Once you are back to where you
began, kneel down and imagine putting the cord back into the
earth along with all the energy that you raised in your working.
Always do the grounding exercise on pages 28–29.

Before you cast your Circle for your spell work you will need to puri-
fy your body. Have a bath or shower (do not use hot water if it will make
you drowsy; see pages 26–27). Put on some clean and comfortable cloth-
ing, preferably without loose sleeves. Loose sleeves and long hair have a
strange attraction to candle flame, so you should roll up your sleeves and
wear your hair back. Do your mirror exercises to ground and center yourself (see pages 28–29) and then enter your Circle space.

Now you are ready to cast your Circle. Until you feel completely comfortable in your space, use some salty water to cleanse the perimeter of
your Circle. Walking clockwise in the northern hemisphere and anticlockwise in the southern hemisphere, sprinkle the water around the
edges of your Circle. Put the bowl back on your table and sit or stand in
the center of your Circle, imagining a line of blue light where you have
sprinkled your salty water. Focus on this blue light, imagining it becom-
ing a deeper, bolder blue. Make the light go down to the ground and rise
up to the ceiling. This is now your Circle space for spellcraft.

Where and When

# Timing your Spells

The moon, the position of the planets and the cycles of nature have a lot to do with the timing of your spells. Full moon is traditionally one of the most effective times to do any type of magic. It is thought that the fullness of the moon relates to a raised level of psychic energy, which can be harnessed for spell casting.

Full moon is the time for healing spells and the making of charm bags to attract love and protection. It is also a good time to cut any herbs you may be growing which would be useful for your spells. The new moon phase is the perfect time to seek inspiration and guidance about a new project, relationship or career.

Spells that deal with the ending of things, such as a relationship or a job, should be done during the waning of the moon (when the moon's light is decreasing).

The energy of each planet is linked to a particular day of the week. Tap into these energies for a successful outcome for your particular spell.

| Day of the week | Planet | Type of energy |
| --- | --- | --- |
| Sunday | Sun | Hope, illumination |
| Monday | Moon | Dreams, shadows |
| Tuesday | Mars | War, enemies |
| Wednesday | Mercury | Intellect, communication |
| Thursday | Jupiter | Money, social gatherings |
| Friday | Venus | Love, friendships |
| Saturday | Saturn | Legal matters, home |

Also consider the energy of each season. If you are doing a spell in Spring, you will be dealing with highly unpredictable and unstable energy. However, this is often the best time to impose your own will on the cosmos. Summer is a much calmer energy, useful for long term and more serious spells where you would like success to be predictable.

In Autumn, the energy is starting to wane and it is time to start storing for Winter, so concentrate on healing spells and those that aid the "harvest" — for example, spells to bring home rewards safely.

Winter's energy goes underground, and this is the best time to look at the past and see where you are going in life and perhaps start thinking of new plans and ideas for Spring. Winter is the time for contemplation, for looking at your successes and failures and for working out a strategy for the new year. Spells that link into Winter's energy are usually those that seek guidance or inspiration for new paths.

# Sending energy to an endangered area

Here is a spell to show you how to put it all together, an example of all the aspects of spell casting that we have talked about. For this spell, it is important that you do all the preparation work and follow each step very carefully.

First, gather all the information about the endangered area you wish to help save — in particular, find pictures of the area and, if you wish, pictures of the people who are on site protesting the threat to the area.

Where and When

Once you have gathered enough information to feel that you are familiar with the area and the issues at stake do your pre-spell casting preparations (see pages 26–29 and 34–37). Only then do the following spell, on a Tuesday:

* put a picture of the area on the floor in the center of the Circle, and your favorite stone in the earth quarter of your Circle;

* walk around the edges of the Circle (clockwise in the northern hemisphere; anticlockwise in the southern hemisphere), beating a branch or stick rhythmically on the floor and imagining you are helping the custodians of the land protect the area by keeping harmful forces away from the perimeters of the endangered area;

* hum, chant or start a slow rhythmic dance as you walk around the Circle. Feel the energy rising within you;

* when the energy feels at the height of its strength, bring your branch or stick down heavily to the floor in the earth section of your Circle, near your stone, imagining the protective energy you have generated running down the branch or stick into the ground and traveling to the area in need.

Once you have finished your spell, do not forget to give thanks to the earth quarter. Imagine the blue light around the edges of your Circle fading to nothing, then ground and center yourself (see pages 28–29).

Where and When

# Friends and Enemies

## Finding new friends ~ a popularity spell

There are times when school or work can be a lonely and unhappy place. Sometimes you may feel that everything you do is wrong, or that you haven't a friend in the world. Try to remember that you are a very powerful person and that you are, despite these feelings, able to make a change.

To help you feel that you can make a difference, put together the following spell bag and let it give you some relief from the negativity around you. The spell is designed to help you become popular or at least find one or two good friends, and involves making a simple cloth bag containing some special ingredients that are designed to attract friendships.

By making this spell bag, you will be inviting a powerful energy to help you reconnect with the people around you and to help others see your good qualities.

You will need to carry the spell bag with you until you feel that the energy around you at school or work is changing for the better. Make sure that you do not show the bag to anyone else. It is important that the energy in the bag remains strong and focused on you. Showing others a spell you have worked on can sometimes have the undesired effect of draining some of the energy you have put into it. However, if you find that the spell works for you, you can still share the instructions with friends on how to make their own spell bags.

On a Friday evening, after you have bathed, grounded and centered yourself and set up your Circle space, cut a light pink circle of cloth big enough to hold the following ingredients:

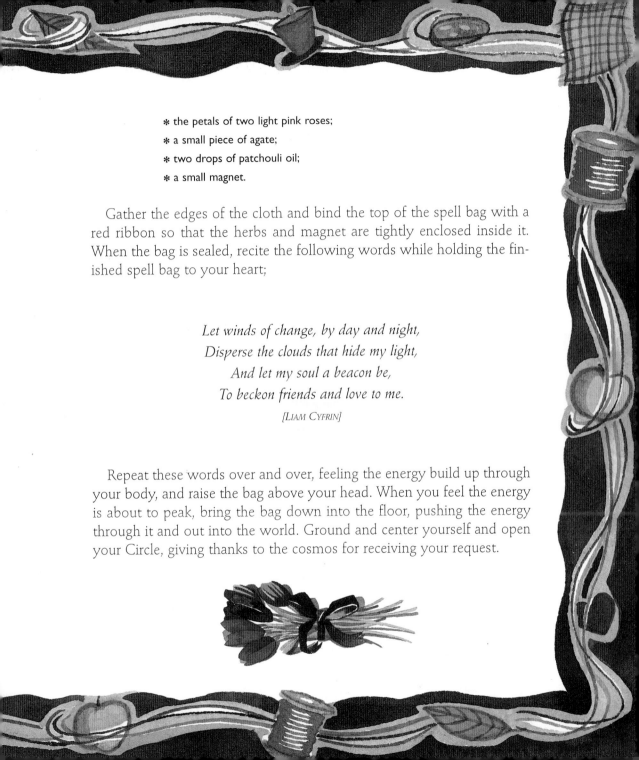

* the petals of two light pink roses;
* a small piece of agate;
* two drops of patchouli oil;
* a small magnet.

Gather the edges of the cloth and bind the top of the spell bag with a red ribbon so that the herbs and magnet are tightly enclosed inside it. When the bag is sealed, recite the following words while holding the finished spell bag to your heart;

*Let winds of change, by day and night,*
*Disperse the clouds that hide my light,*
*And let my soul a beacon be,*
*To beckon friends and love to me.*

[LIAM CYFRIN]

Repeat these words over and over, feeling the energy build up through your body, and raise the bag above your head. When you feel the energy is about to peak, bring the bag down into the floor, pushing the energy through it and out into the world. Ground and center yourself and open your Circle, giving thanks to the cosmos for receiving your request.

# Helping friends in need

Casting spells for other people is a useful way of helping your immediate community. When you are asked to cast a spell for someone, take time to find out what your friend really wants. For example, if you are asked to cast a money spell, be sure to find out whether it is the money itself that your friend wants, or something that the money can buy.

If you are thinking of doing a healing spell, make sure that the person receiving the healing really wants to be well. Directing energy is an important skill to develop. There is a theory that people become sick for a particular karmic purpose, and you may need to use your intuition to work out whether you would be interfering with your patient's own true will.

If you are casting a spell for someone, it is a really good idea, unless you are dealing with an emergency, always to ask the permission of the person involved before doing any casting. If you don't, you may find that the person feels, despite your best intentions, as if their privacy has been invaded.

## Spell Tip

Remember to follow two golden rules when casting
spells for your friends:
* Wait to be asked OR
* Ask permission first before casting a spell.

For sending energy to a friend, there is a specific technique that is effective for directing energy. Sit on a mat or a comfortable chair in your special space after you have cast a Circle, and imagine that each breath you draw in is colored in a gentle blue shade. The blue signifies harmony with your intention. If you wish to cast a healing or protective energy around

Friends and Enemies

your friend, imagine this intention mingling with your indrawn breath. With your next exhalation, imagine that your breath and your intention are a particular type of energy force, such as healing energy or love.

Now, imagine as you exhale that the energy is coming out of your hands. Practice this until you feel a strong flow of energy in your hands. Rub the palms of your hand together to increase the energy flow. When the energy feels as strong as you can make it, imagine your friend standing in front of you, looking well or well protected, and send the energy into that image through your hands.

Another useful thing you can do for your friends is to make a spell box for their birthdays or for special occasions (see pages 32–33), putting all your good wishes for them in the box. You could also make a spell bracelet (see pages 46–47).

Spell Tip

Remember that all spells performed in a Circle (after you have bathed or showered (see pages 26–27), grounded and centered yourself (see pages 28–29) and cast your Circle (see pages 34–37) in your special space), will work more reliably. If working in a Circle, don't forget to open the Circle when you have finished spell casting, as well as grounding and centering yourself.

# Making a spell bracelet to honor your friendship

Spell bracelets are a powerful way of sharing your energies with a friend and of strengthening your bonds. To make one you will need:

* a tapestry or embroidery needle;
* a spool of cotton or silk thread (choose a dark color, like red, blue, purple, or forest green);
* a selection of small images (make sure they do not have sharp edges) and beads (of any shape or size);
* a button;
* a clipboard (or a length of board with a nail at one end);
* some adhesive tape and scissors.

**1** To make the bracelet, measure out eight strands of cotton or silk thread, each 30 inches (75 cm) in length. Measure out another strand of thread 60 inches (150 cm) in length. Bunch up the eight strands and fold them in half. Use the longer strand of cotton to tie a knot just below where the strands curve over, so that you are making a loop. You will be attaching a button at the other end of the bracelet, so make sure that the loop you make is big enough to allow the button to pass through snugly. Stitch through the knot you have made a couple of times, using the long end of the 60 inch (150 cm) thread.

**2** Sew a figure eight stitch around the small buttonhole loop. To do this, sew through the middle of your threads from the right and then loop round to sew through the middle of your threads from the left. Continue this stitch until

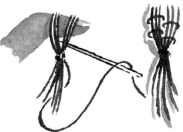

Friends and Enemies

you have completed the full circuit around the small buttonhole loop. This is going to be your basic stitch throughout the whole bracelet.

3 Once you have finished the buttonhole, secure it to the clipboard or loop it over the nail on your length of board. Holding all the threads securely, continue the figure eight stitch down the center of your bracelet for seven stitches. Peel off two strands of thread and thread your charm or bead onto them. Use adhesive tape to keep them away from the main bunch of threads, which you will continue to stitch together with the figure eight stitch. When you have gone down the center threads for the full length of the bead, pick up the strands taped away from the center and include the threads with the figure eight stitch. Continue separating two strands at a time to thread in your beads until the bracelet is the length you require (usually between 7 and 9 inches (18–24 cm)).

4 When you want to finish, separate the central bunch of threads into half and cut one half off diagonally. Thread your button on the remaining threads and loop the threads around so that they meet and slightly overlap the ends of the threads you have cut. Continue with the figure eight stitch over the join and up until the button feels secure.

5 When finished, sprinkle some salted water over the bracelet to give it a final cleansing. Then give it to your friend.

Friends and Enemies

# Stopping negative energy from hurting you

The first step to stopping negative energy from hurting you is to set up a shield of protection. Draw a circle on a piece of cardboard, a sheet of pine or balsa wood or tin, and draw, paint or paste decorations on your miniature shield, leaving the middle clear. Write your name in the middle of the shield and draw or paint the protection rune ( ᚹ ) 13 times in a circle around your name.

Cut out two circles of blue natural fabric, such as cotton, linen or silk, and sew the shield between the two pieces of fabric, keeping the shield from sight. Tuck in a leaf from a mint bush and carry this shield with you whenever you anticipate being in a situation where you might attract negative energy (see also pages 60–67).

## Simple Spell

**Purchase a bag of dried juniper berries and string them onto a cotton thread long enough to wear around your neck. Wear this necklace under your clothes whenever you feel negative energies affecting you. Juniper berries are traditionally considered very reliable at dissolving negative energy that is directed at you.**

Another spell that can help you stop negative energy from hurting you is one that heightens your own feeling of inner strength. To do this, find a picture of the type of strength you need — for example, a beautiful eagle or a hawk, which is the symbol of clear vision. Draw or photocopy the picture if you find it in a book, or cut it out if the picture is in a magazine. As you draw, photocopy or cut the image, say the following words:

*This image holds the strength I seek,*
*I heed not words the heartless speak;*
*The image and my soul are one,*
*And those who'll wound me number none.*

[LIAM CYFRIN]

If someone's cruel words are giving you grief, try the following spell. Only write down the exact words you find hurtful. Get a small bowl and pour into it a whole packet of rock salt. Wedge a candle firmly into the salt and then light the candle. Burn the piece of paper and imagine the words having no effect in the world, as if they had never been said.

Now concentrate on the feelings you had when hearing those words. As you are focusing on your feeling of hurt, guilt or pain, imagine the emotion being contained in a blue or green sphere that is spinning in front of your heart. Imagine the sphere getting smaller and smaller until you can no longer see it. By contracting the sphere "containing" your feeling to nothing, you will soon feel that the hurt and pain have also disappeared.

Spell Tip

When you have finished with the salt used in this last spell, sweep it into a special small box and keep it for any other magic work you may wish to do. This is a rare example of being able to reuse spell ingredients.

# Dealing with difficult people

Projecting a sense of generosity or goodwill is an effective way of dealing with difficult people. It is one of the cleanest ways of handling people who seem petty or who are acting in a self-centered manner.

If you are finding someone difficult to communicate with because they are angry or frustrated, carry a piece of green obsidian with you to help protect you from their negative emotions. When talking with a difficult person, imagine a sphere, the color of the green obsidian (a clear, light, green-blue color), shining between you. Imagine that all the words you are saying to each other are being heard through the green-blue sphere and the sphere is filtering the harshness away from the words, making it easier and easier for you to talk to each other.

Never be tempted, even as a joke, to stick pins or other sharp objects into the image of a person, in the form of photograph or a poppet or wax

doll, as a way of stopping or "binding" them from doing any harm to you or to those you love. Never tamper with the free will of another person unless you are prepared to pay a heavy price.

A safer and even more potent type of spell is one where you cast a protective shield over the person being affected by the difficult person (see pages 48–49 and 60–63). These types of spells are much stronger than any attempts to bind

## Simple Spell

When going into a difficult meeting, wear a ring set with a ruby to attract
kindness from the people you are dealing with.

a person, because binding spells mean that you have to link into the
destructive energy of that other person, creating a downward spiral of
negative energy that will draw you in when your guard is down.

A spell to encourage a sense of protection from a troublesome person
for yourself or your friend is one that involves surrounding a photograph
of yourself or your friend with a circle of salt. Make sure that the circle
has no gaps in it; you will need to use a fair amount of salt. You may leave
the photograph and salt set up in your special space for as long as you
wish to keep away from the troublesome person. If you wish to improve
relations with the person, place a circle of flowers (those without thorns)
and sweet things to eat around his or her photograph. This will encourage a happier energy to exist for that person.

# Falling In and Out of Love

## Working love spells

Love spells help you nurture your relationships and improve their quality. The spells that work best are often those that attract compatible people to each other. It is fine to ask to meet your true love, but it is not ethical to use spellcraft to make someone fall in love with you — or anyone else. Doing so can be categorized as black magic, because you are interfering with a person's free will.

Many traditional love spells involve the simple symbol of the heart. Cut the shape of the heart out of some lemon rind and carry it in a cotton bag in your pocket, and you will meet a new love within one cycle of the moon. Other fruits and foods that can be used in a love spell include:

| | |
|---|---|
| Apple | Ginger |
| Banana | Mango |
| Cherry | Orange |
| Chocolate | Peaches |
| Cinnamon | Pineapple |
| Clove | Strawberries |

In a small pan, boil a quarter of a cup of orange juice, seven cloves and a pinch of cinnamon and sweet paprika until only a small amount is left. As you are boiling the liquid and breathing in the scent, think of the type of love you wish to attract. Think in terms of what type of person you would like your loved one to be. Once you have only a thimble sized volume, decant it into a small bottle that you can wear around your neck. You will meet your new love within one cycle of the moon.

A red rose is also a powerful symbol of love, and is often used in love spells, since it was believed to be the flower of Venus, the goddess of love. Carrying rose petals in a small linen bag was thought to be a way of attracting love to you. Even eating rose petals was thought to give a person some of the rose's beauty. The petals of other flowers that can be used in a love spell include the following:

| Flower | Type of love attracted |
|--------|------------------------|
| Carnation | Lively love |
| Magnolia | Loyal love |
| Orange blossom | Lucky love |
| Gardenia | Healing love |
| Violet | Fulfilling love |

Rose oil, called Rose Otto (rosa damascena), is the most expensive aromatherapy oil, yet there are other more affordable oils that have traditionally attracted love to their user. Sprinkle a few drops of one of the oils opposite on a red candle with the words "New Love" carved down the side. After burning the whole candle, you will attract a new love within three cycles of the moon.

Cardamom
Carnation
Cinnamon
Clove
Dill
Gardenia

Hibiscus
Jasmine
Mugwort
Patchouli
Ylang-ylang

# Spells to find out who will be your boyfriend

There are three varieties of spells to help you find out who will be your next boyfriend, or your husband. This usually means finding out who is attracted to you. The first type of spell gives you a name. The second type of spell prepares you in such a way that after you complete your preparations the first person whom you meet or who makes a certain comment is going to be your next love. The third type of spell gives you visual contact with your future love through your dreams (see page 56). Spells to generally attract love to you can be found on pages 52–53.

A simple way of finding out who is attracted to you is by peeling an apple or an orange at the time of the new moon. The trick is to peel the whole fruit in one go, so that the spiral of apple or orange peel is unbroken from the top to the bottom of the fruit. Walk around in a circle three times (clockwise in the northern hemisphere and anticlockwise in the southern hemisphere) holding the apple or orange peel in your hands and say the following words continuously (this is called saying a mantra):

*Let nature's fruit and ancient art*
*Spell out his name who'll win my heart;*
*Let nature's fruit and ancient spell*
*Bespeak his name who'll love me well.*

[LIAM CYFRIN]

When you have finished walking around three times, throw the peel down in the center of the circle. See if it seems to spell out a male name. Do not worry if the peel breaks on impact or if the name is not fully spelt out. If you can make out three letters (or even the first letter), this will give you an indication of the name of someone attracted to you.

The next type of spell dates back many centuries. There are quite a number of versions, such as running around your local cemetery on St Valentine's Eve saying a magical charm. The idea is that your future husband will be compelled to come to the graveyard to show himself to you. However, this is not necessarily the ideal place for a first date.

Try this spell instead — pick a red rose at the Summer solstice and keep it until the Winter solstice. If the flower does not fall apart, place it in a buttonhole in your jacket when going to a church or other spiritual place. The first male to admire the rose will be your husband.

# True love and dream magic

Dream magic is best practiced during a full moon. If you seek information about a new love or friend, cleanse your pillows of any previous negative energies by airing and fluffing them in the light of the full moon.

Write down what you wish to know about your love life, such as who will be your own true love or your next love, or how to improve your relationship with a particular friend or love. Write down your wish in a special dream journal. This can be a small exercise book that you keep only for recording your dreams. Dreams give us important information about ourselves and those close to us, and can often offer solutions about any troublesome relationships we might be having.

Before you settle down in bed, place a sprig of rosemary under your pillow to make sure you don't have any nightmares. Also keep a sage leaf under your pillow for three nights in a row to encourage dreams of your future love.

Recite the following charm three times just before you fall asleep and see if you get a sign of who your lover will be:

*May sweetest dreams and second sight*
*Reveal to me my love this night*
*His face, his form — no feature miss —*
*His voice, his touch, his smile, his kiss;*
*May sweetest dreams and second sight*
*Unite me with my love this night.*

[LIAM CYFRIN]

Keep a record of your dreams for the next three nights and see what inspirations and people come into your dreams.

You might notice that you have very vivid dreams after casting Circles and doing other types of spells. It is a good idea to keep a record of what you dream after casting a Circle, as you will often be rewarded with some interesting insights.

Falling In and Out of Love

# Falling out of love ~ spells to help

There are a number of healing rituals that can be used to help say good-bye to someone you have cared for. If you are suffering the irrevocable breakdown of a relationship, gather together a photograph of your love, a few sprigs of rosemary, a white candle and a bowl containing some sand or soil. Anoint the candle with a fragrance that reminds you of your love and carve their name down the side of the candle.

Burn the candle and simply watch the flame. Imagine the flame burning away any pain caused by the breakup. Concentrate on the candle for as long as you wish, then save it if it has not burnt all the way down, and use it for the same ceremony on the next two nights.

Even if you are pleased with the breakup, consider having this ceremony. It is a great way of honoring the person who has passed through your life. By honoring this person you are also honoring yourself, and you may receive some interesting insights on the relationship that will help you to build better and stronger ones in the future.

If you are faced with someone forcing unwanted attention on you, try the following visualization. (The idea of this spell is to imagine a cloak of invisibility wrapping around you which has an effect only on the person you wish to discourage. What will happen is that the person you seek to discourage will not be able to focus on you — they will not be able to see you clearly, and this will give you time to move away from them.)

Imagine a white full length cloak wrapped around your body, with a hood held over your face. Imagine that the cloak is held together by a

clasp or brooch. The clasp or brooch must be real — one that you like or have specially bought for this purpose.

At full moon, bring into your special place the clasp or brooch, a bag of sea or rock salt and a piece of paper and a pen. Place your clasp or brooch on your table and sprinkle the salt in a circle around the object. Draw a picture of your unwanted friend, writing his or her name underneath it, and then place the picture outside the circle.

Leave the objects on the table. If after three days they are still set up as you have left them, your clasp will be charged with the cloak of invisibility and you will be able to evade the unwanted attentions of that particular person whenever you wear the clasp or carry it with you in a small white cloth bag.

However, if the objects have been disturbed (if the photograph was slightly moved or the salt grains shifted by a vibration in the floorboards), check with yourself why you do not want this particular person as a friend or love. Are you overlooking something? Could they turn out to be a good friend for you?

Falling In and Out of Love

# Protecting Yourself

## Personal safety spells

One aspect of being an effective spell caster is that by believing in and caring about yourself, you do not drift into unsafe situations. However, there are times when circumstances will require you to think more about your protection — for instance, when walking home or traveling on public transport late at night. Whatever the potential dangers you *can* direct your own destiny to a certain extent. Try these two spells.

When walking home at night, imagine two black panthers walking noiselessly beside you. Imagine that the three of you are the most dangerous thing walking on the street. Another useful spell is to imagine a blue circle of light shining around your body. Visualize this line expanding into a sheet of thin blue light that envelops you in a soft cocoon. Once enveloped into this safe space, you will still be able to move about, but other people may find it hard to focus on you clearly; this will give you the opportunity to move out of the range of the unwanted attention.

When you are feeling safe, remember to earth the blue cocoon into the ground by sweeping your arms up to the top of your cocoon and "collecting" the light into your hands. Bring your hands down to the ground and visualize the energy running safely into the ground.

A talisman was apparently once given to King Solomon for psychic protection. To create a similar talisman for yourself, write the following square of letters on a piece of paper and tie to your watch band, or place in a locket worn on a bracelet around your left wrist:

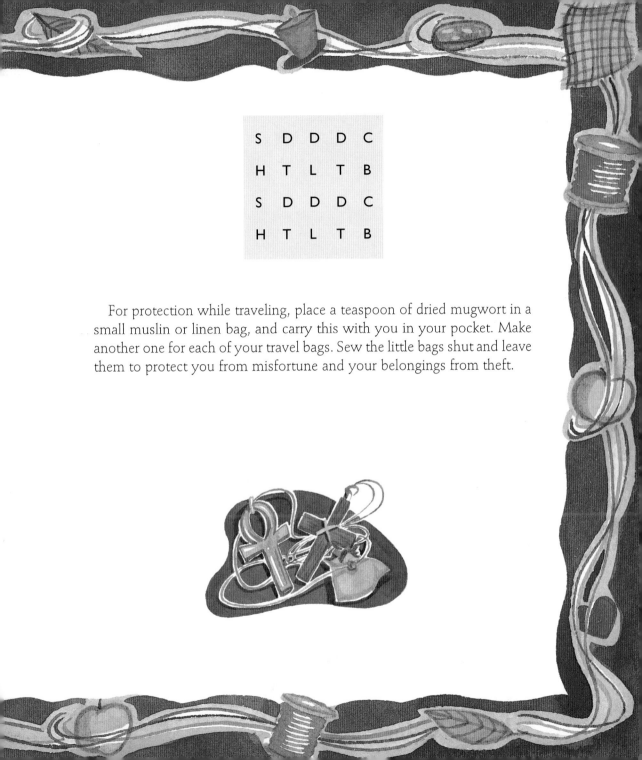

```
S  D  D  D  C
H  T  L  T  B
S  D  D  D  C
H  T  L  T  B
```

For protection while traveling, place a teaspoon of dried mugwort in a small muslin or linen bag, and carry this with you in your pocket. Make another one for each of your travel bags. Sew the little bags shut and leave them to protect you from misfortune and your belongings from theft.

# Making a charm bag for protection

Charm bags have been used in protection spells from time immemorial. They are very simple to make and contain stones, herbs, words, amulets or talismans which contain a certain form of psychic energy or vibration. For a protection spell, you will need to collect the following objects for your charm bag:

* a quartz crystal, symbolizing earth;
* an aromatic herb, such as dill or garlic, symbolizing air;
* a cone shell, symbolizing water;
* a pinch of cayenne pepper, symbolizing fire.

Place the stone and the shell in the center of a circular piece of natural fiber, such as silk, linen or cotton, which has been dyed red. Sprinkle the pepper and the herb (either dill or the white papery skin of a clove of garlic). In running stitch, sew around the cloth about 1/3 inch (1 cm) from the edge of the circle with a length of red thread. When you have sewn right around the edge, tie the two ends of the thread together and gently pull the thread so that the bag slowly closes over the top of the objects. Now you may wish to knot the thread so that the bag is kept permanently closed.

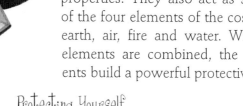

All the ingredients in the bag are traditionally said to have protective properties. They also act as symbols of the four elements of the cosmos — earth, air, fire and water. When the elements are combined, the ingredients build a powerful protective force.

Light a red candle at each of the four compass points in your special space and say the following words:

| Direction in the Northern Hemisphere | Direction in the Southern Hemisphere | Words to say |
| --- | --- | --- |
| North | South | Powers of Earth<br>Bless my charm and let it protect me from all harm |
| East | West | Powers of Air<br>Bless my charm and let it protect me from all harm |
| South | North | Powers of Fire<br>Bless my charm and let it protect me from all harm |
| West | East | Powers of Water<br>Bless my charm and let it protect me from all harm |

Hold the charm bag in your hands, and with closed eyes visualize brilliant red energy glowing around it, growing stronger and radiating out to fill your special space. Blow out the candles, giving thanks to each element for its energy, and carry the charm bag with you whenever you feel the need for protection.

# Protecting your space

To strengthen the feeling of protection provided by your safe space, consider casting a permanent Circle to protect against interruptions and harmful thoughts. Just remember to open the Circle whenever you need to enter or leave the space. See pages 34–37 on how to cast your Circle.

If you sense that your home does not feel safe, you can cast a cleansing Circle to prevent any negative energy from entering it. Walk around your home (in a clockwise direction in the northern hemisphere; in an anticlockwise direction in the southern hemisphere), while sprinkling salted water in front of you with a sprig of rosemary.

You can further protect your place from negative influences by sealing all the windows and doors of your home, particularly those in your special space and in the space where you dream. Sprinkle some salt water around the front of each window and all doors leading to the outside world, and leave in front of each window and above each outside door a small bunch of fresh or dried basil, parsley and dill tied together with a length of red ribbon. Place above the door leading to your special space or your bedroom a cross, a quartered circle, a pentagram (a five pointed star enclosed in a circle with one point uppermost) or a hexagram (a six pointed star enclosed in a circle), drawn on a piece of paper in red ink.

If you are handy with a needle and do quite a bit of sewing, whether of garments, embroidery or cross-stitch work, you can keep all your unused and discarded threads in one jar. Each time you place some thread in the jar, say under your breath the following words:

*These tangled threads, this ancient charm,*
*Shall guard from hardship, guard from harm.*
*No ill may pass the web that spreads,*
*From this small nest of tangled threads.*

[LIAM CYFRIN]

When the jar is completely filled with threads, seal the lid with red wax or red-colored tape and place the jar at the highest point in your house, such as on top of a rafter or a tall piece of furniture. This will keep your household safe from undue hardship and harm.

## Simple Spell

Another useful spell is to place near your front door a piece of carnelian, which you have held while visualizing your house protected from burglary. Place another piece of carnelian at your back door.

# Protecting your belongings

There are plenty of spells for protection against being robbed, many of which involve selecting a herb, stone or symbol and placing it with the things you wish to protect. Scan the herbs and stones in the tables below and choose those that call to you. If none do, concentrate on your purpose and see if another stone or herb comes to mind. The table lists a selection that would be suitable for use in a protection spell.

| Herbs | Stones |
| --- | --- |
| Cinnamon sticks | Bloodstone |
| Cardamom seeds | Tiger's eye |
| Cloves (whole) | Amethyst |
| Nutmeg (whole) | Jade |
| Ginger (a dried slice) | Carnelian |
| Rosemary | Quartz crystal |
| Bay leaves | Aventurine |
| Basil leaves | Garnet |
| Dill seeds | Hematite |
| Juniper berries (whole) | Topaz |

Place the object in front of you and concentrate on an image of your belongings; imagine they are invisible to anyone but yourself. If you have chosen a stone, hold it in your hand while you visualize the image of your belongings not being seen by anyone who wants to steal them. If you have chosen a herb, place a small amount in a little bag. Hold these while you imagine the success of your spell. At the same time as your visualization, chant the following words:

Protecting Yourself

*By wind and flame, by stone and sea,*
*I banish all who thieves would be.*
*That which I own their eyes won't see,*
*That which is mine remain with me.*

[LIAM CYFRIN]

By holding your herb, stone or symbol as you visualize, you are charging the objects with the positive outcome or success of your wish. Keep the herb or stone near, or in, your purse, luggage or carry bag. If you wish to keep your journal secret, place the herb or stone on top of the book. A small branch of the dogwood plant lying diagonally across your journal will help to keep it safe from prying eyes.

It is a magical tradition that herbs with sharp edges, such as mistletoe, nettles, thistles (particularly blessed thistle), and those with a sharp taste, such as ginger, cloves and pepper, are protective herbs. For a very simple spell, just have a few sharp edged leaves or a couple of cloves or peppercorns tucked away with your things. If you want to protect your car so it is not booked for being parked over the time limit, imagine a blue light surrounding it and ask that your car be spared from the attentions of a traffic warden. Never abuse this spell, and only use it when you have done your best to find a suitable car parking space.

## ✳ Simple Spell

To discourage the theft of your belongings, burn some incense containing frankincense in an incense holder, passing your purse, wallet, handbag or luggage over the incense stick and through the incense smoke.

Protecting Yourself

# The Art of Spellcraft

## How to work out your own spells

From ancient times, spell casters have believed that every rock, herb, plant, flower, animal, color and other aspects of nature has specific psychic vibrations. These items have become symbols that we can use in our spells to attract what we want in our lives.

In this book you have been introduced to a number of different types of spells. Many of these spells combine objects with the same psychic vibrations to attract such energies as protection, love or money. These spells work on the basis that, if you add similar vibrations together, the same type of energy will be attracted to them.

To work out how many ingredients to use in a spell or how much of an ingredient to include in a spell, many spell casters use planetary correspondences. That is to say, they look at how the planets correspond with particular numbers and types of energy.

| Planet | Magical activity | Corresponding number |
|--------|------------------|----------------------|
| Sun | Friendships, health, obtaining money | 6 |
| Moon | Inspiration, preventing disagreements | 9 |
| Mercury | Success in exams, preventing theft | 8 |
| Venus | Acquiring friends and beauty, love | 7 |
| Mars | Acquiring strength, courage | 5 |
| Jupiter | Gaining success in career | 4 |
| Saturn | Protecting the home | 3 |

## ✳ Simple Spell

You can shield yourself from negative energies by carrying a piece of jet or
onyx with you whenever you expect to see a person who is angry with
you or annoyed at you. These black stones should be washed in salty
water before you use them. If you need to use them for a long period,
remember to give them a wash once a week to clear out the negativity.

Use the table, left, to work out the magic number to suit the purpose
of your spell.

If a spell is to stick to a particular person, the spell ingredients should
ideally include a lock of that person's hair or nail clippings. This kind of
spell works on the basis that physical bits of a person, such as the hair,
nails and blood, contain a magical link to that person. This is called con-
tagious magic, and one of the physical items should be included in the
spell if you wish it to work specifically for a particular person other
than yourself.

Spells can work at many different
levels of power. If you simply combine the right ingredients with the
right psychic vibrations and keep
them with you in a small pouch, the
spell will eventually work in its own
time as an all purpose spell, like one
to protect you from all harm. This is
because you can't possibly know all

the negative things that can be directed toward you, and you don't want to limit the psychic energy created by the spell.

To power the spell along, you sometimes need to give it an added charge. The simplest way of doing this is by visualizing the success of the spell as you are combining your ingredients. Use this method when you want something specific. If you are asking for something big, like meeting your soul mate or getting money for a house, always ask the favor of the four elements to help power your spell along even further. This type of empowerment is called elemental consecration, and it is very easy to achieve. Once you have finished combining your ingredients in a bowl, pouch or other container, and you have visualized your spell's success, pick up the container and pass it over a burning candle (symbolizing fire), a bowl of water (symbolizing water), a semiprecious stone (for example, ironstone, jasper or tiger's eye symbolizing earth), and a burning stick of incense (symbolizing air). You could also use the procedure on page 63.

*Spell Tip*

Never do more than one spell at a time. Direct all your psychic power toward the one purpose, otherwise you may jeopardize the success of any other spells you do at the same time.

The Art of Spellcraft

# Spells from the garden

Herbs, plants and flowers are often used in spells. Certain herbs can be burnt as an essential oil or kept as a bundle in dried form to attract a particular form of energy or to give you protection.

Growing herbs is easy because they generally do not need particularly good soil and they respond well to companion planting. This involves planting together certain flowers, herbs and vegetables that help each other to grow. If you grow your own herbs, gather those you need for a particular spell during the evening at the time of the waxing moon. This will ensure that their psychic energy will be on the rise.

Folklore traditions recommend cutting herbs at full moon if you wish to bring health, and at a waning to a new moon if you wish to get rid of disease. If you wish to use the herbs to assure the success of a new project as it begins, it is recommended you cut the herbs at new moon. It is best to cut with a special knife that you use only for harvesting your herbs for your spells.

Choose one of the herbs from the table opposite to make it into an amulet in the form of a small herb sachet. This can be hung around your neck or your friend's, allowing the body's warmth, particularly that between the breasts, to release the fragrance.

When you have finished making your amulet, sprinkle some chamomile into it to increase its power. If you are seeking good luck, make an amulet containing cinnamon sticks. For love potions, clover can be used to find out who your soul mate will be. For the protection of your family, cumin could also be added to your amulet.

The Art of Spellcraft

| Herb | Magical properties |
|------|-------------------|
| Acorn | success of creative work |
| Angelica | protection against psychic attack |
| Borage | happiness, joy |
| Chamomile | calming, protecting |
| Cinnamon | concentration, focus |
| Dill | dispels negative energies |
| Dogwood | keeps secrets, seals secret journals |
| Dragon's blood | protective, seals sacred manuscripts |
| Fennel | protective, ability to face danger and adversity |
| Frankincense | protective, cleansing |
| Garlic | protective, strengthening |
| Ginger | protective |
| Horehound | aids trust in your intuition |
| Hyssop | protective, particularly of the house |
| Jasmine | psychic protection |
| Lavender | increases awareness |
| Lovage | attracts romance |
| Mistletoe | protective, promotes harmony |
| Sage | wisdom, cleansing evil |
| Verbena | enhances lucid dreaming |

You may put together a pot pourri of different herbs to create a protective or enhancing atmosphere in your special room, home, school or place of work. Some pleasing combinations include:

* rose petals, lavender, cloves and cinnamon, for love;
* orange peel, nutmeg, cloves and thyme, for psychic awareness;
* dill, rosemary, bay leaf and black peppercorns, for protection;
* ginger, bergamot and cloves, for money.

The Art of Spellcraft

# Lucky charms

Lucky charms come in many shapes or forms. Since ancient times, the belief has been that it is purely a matter of chance whether you are born lucky or unlucky. Over time, certain symbols, including precious and semiprecious stones, have gained the reputation of being able to attract good luck or shield a person from bad luck. A list of stones that are lucky for people who were born under a particular astrological sign developed over the years (see the table opposite).

A "charm" traditionally meant a single word or phrase spoken or written down on paper, parchment, wood or even engraved upon a metal object. It could be as simple as a phrase that encapsulated what you wanted, such as "good grades". When reciting a charm today, it is important that you put as much feeling into speaking the word or phrase as possible. As you recite, imagine an aura of luck shining around you.

There are also a number of objects traditionally considered to be good luck charms, such as the horseshoe. It is thought that the horseshoe represents a new or crescent moon. If you have a horseshoe, attach it above your front door or above the door leading to your special space; make sure that it is displayed with its points rising up, so that the luck can fall into the "U" shape.

Charms can also be natural objects, such as acorns, juniper berries, or bayberry bark. Bayberries, as well as cedar or pine, are reputed to attract money, while an acorn symbolizes new hope and juniper berries shield a person from negative energies. Certain gems and crystals are believed to be lucky. An example of this is moonstone, particularly if it is bathed with the light of the new moon as you charge it with your wish for luck.

The Art of Spellcraft

| What sun sign are you? | What are your lucky stones? |
| --- | --- |
| Aries<br>_20th March to 20th April_ | Bloodstone, opal, diamond |
| Taurus<br>_21st April to 21st May_ | Amethyst, moss agate, sapphire |
| Gemini<br>_22nd May to 21st June_ | Lapis lazuli, moonstone, emerald |
| Cancer<br>_22nd June to 22nd July_ | Cornelian, pearl, ruby |
| Leo<br>_23rd July to 23rd August_ | Amber, black onyx, peridot |
| Virgo<br>_24th August to 23rd September_ | Jade, sardonyx, jasper |
| Libra<br>_24th September to 23rd October_ | Chrysolite, coral, tourmaline |
| Scorpio<br>_24th October to 23rd November_ | Malachite, topaz, aquamarine |
| Sagittarius<br>_24th November to 21st December_ | Turquoise, moonstone, topaz |
| Capricorn<br>_22nd December to 20th January_ | Jet, garnet, ruby |
| Aquarius<br>_21st January to 18th February_ | Jade, amethyst, sapphire |
| Pisces<br>_19th February to 19th March_ | Opal, pearl, moonstone |

The Art of Spellcraft

# Money magic spells

What is money magic? This type of magic includes spells that help you get money for a particular purpose. Many traditional spells work only if you focus solely on your immediate needs — what you need now. Some spell casters believe that money magic does not work if your wish is for something you would just like to have, rather than something you really need. However, as long as you are not greedy about your wants, a money spell may still work for you if you desire some luxury item.

The predominant color to use for money magic spells is green. Look for green stones, candles, cloth and ribbon. See the table on page 73 for herbs, plants and flowers that are useful for attracting money. The best time to do money magic spells is on a Thursday evening, because this day of the week is ruled by Jupiter, a planet reputed to affect our riches and heartfelt desires. Choose carefully in which season to do your spell (see the table below):

| Season | Seasonal psychic energy | Type of money magic spell |
|--------|-------------------------|---------------------------|
| Spring | Quick return, but the result may be unpredictable; risky ventures and gambles | Best to cast spells for small wishes, like a holiday to relieve stress |
| Summer | Reliable result; strong, mature energy | Best to cast spells for medium sized wishes, like a new car |
| Autumn | Excellent result; harvest time | Best to cast spells for large sized wishes, like a scholarship |
| Winter | Slow return; energy has gone underground | Best to cast spells for long term wishes, like a home |

As with all spells, it is important that you concentrate on only one request at a time. A simple spell that you can do to attract money for a specific purpose is to make a small charm bag to hang around your neck or carry with you in your pocket. You will need:

* a piece of circular green, or predominantly green, fabric;
* a thin green cord and a needle with an eye large enough to be threaded with the cord;
* a green candle;
* a stone, such as amethyst, turquoise, carnelian or green adventurine;
* a piece of cedar or pine;
* a coin of the highest denomination issued in your country;
* four cloves.

Gather these ingredients and set yourself up in your special space. Bring with you a thick piece of cardboard, matches, a blunt knife and some scissors.

Light the green candle and imagine that you are attracting a sense of abundance and prosperity to yourself. Tip the candle so that the green wax drips onto your piece of cardboard. Make the drip large enough so that you can write on the wax the purpose of the money spell. You may simply choose to use the word "Computer" or "$10,000". Try to keep your green candle burning until you have finished the spell.

Whilst the wax is cooling, sew the cord around the edges of the fabric in a simple running stitch, and place your other ingredients in the center of the circular piece of fabric. Once the wax is cool, write your special word on the wax with the needle and peel it off the cardboard and place it in the bag. Draw the fabric shut and tie a knot to keep the bag closed.

With an intake of breath, imagine that you are breathing strong energy from the fire of your candle down into your hands. Feel your hands vibrate with power, and allow that power to be transferred into the bag. Exhale, and feel that the energy has been imbedded into your charm.

The Art of Spellcraft

# Glossary

AMULET: an object with magical properties of protection.

ANOINT: to rub oil on an object, such as a candle.

BLACK MAGIC: a general term referring to a form of magic that seeks to manipulate or control others.

CENTERING: bringing the body's energy into a central column running through the body so that the energy is concentrated and focused toward a magical purpose, such as a spell.

CHARM: a magical word or words that can be used as a protection or to attract certain energy.

CIRCLE: a sacred space, usually thought of as a sphere of energy created when the Circle is cast.

CONE OF POWER: raising the energy within the Circle to a peak that can then be directed to the purpose in mind.

GROUNDING: connecting the body's energy with that of the earth.

INVOKE: to summon a spirit or energy form into oneself.

KARMA: an Eastern concept that you are liable in the future for any past wrongs.

MANTRA: a repeated word or phrase which is taken from sacred texts, or phrases affirming a particular quality, such as "I am strong, I am powerful". The words are repeated indefinitely to help a person quieten their mind to become more in touch with their soul.

PENTACLE: a five pointed star made of metal or other material that is the symbol of the four elements and the spirit and can be worn as a protection. The pentacle is also an important elemental tool symbolizing earth. If it is upright, with the point uppermost, the pentacle is a symbol of Wicca (an old English name for the practice of witchcraft). If it is upside down, with the point at the bottom, the pentacle is usually a symbol of Satanism.

PENTAGRAM: a five pointed figure that is used as a blessing.

POPPET: a simple cloth doll made in the image of a human. It can be stuffed with items from a particular person to help personalize it for magical purposes.

PSYCHIC ENERGY: a form of energy that can be felt when focusing on spiritual qualities within yourself, or the Earth and Her creations, such as the rocks, plants or animals.

RUNES: magical symbols which were first used by ancient Nordic and Germanic cultures. These symbols can be used for divination (seeking the future and understanding the past) and are inscribed on talismans and amulets.

TALISMAN: an object charged with a specific magical purpose.

WITCH: traditionally a female witch. However, in modern times this term refers to both male and female witches.

The following tables show you what various objects symbolize in terms of psychic energy:

* the elements (page 13);
* the Seasons (page 76);
* colors of candles (page 18);
* aromatherapy oils (pages 18; 27);
* stones (page 21);
* stones for luck (page 75);
* trees and leaves (page 24);
* days of the week (page 38);
* food and flowers for love (pages 52–53);
* herbs and stones for protection (page 66);
* herbs generally (page 73).

Glossary

This edition published by Prentice Hall
by arrangement with Lansdowne Publishing

ISBN 0-7352-0323-7

Published by Lansdowne Publishing Pty Ltd
Sydney NSW 2000, Australia

Commissioned by: Deborah Nixon
Production Manager: Kristy Nelson
Project Co-ordinator: Alexandra Nahlous
Copy Editor: Avril Janks
Designer: Sue Rawkins
Illustrator: Sue Ninham

Set in Stempel Schneidler, Gill Sans and Girls Are Weird on Quark Xpress
Printed in Singapore by Tien Wah Press (Pte) Ltd

Prentice Hall
Paramus, NJ 07652
http://www.phdirect.com